Baylor Prayers

Dan B. Scott
Foreword by Headmaster Scott Wilson

Parson's
Porch
Books

Baylor Prayers

Dan Scott
Foreword by Headmaster Scott Wilson

Parson's Porch Books

Baylor Prayers

Copyright © 2012 by Dan B. Scott

ISBN: 978-1-936912-62-9   Softcover

This book was printed in the United States of America.

Cover Art Credit: Baylor School Alumni Chapel by Wayne Wu, AWS, 1986.

To order additional copies of this book, contact:

Parson's Porch & Company
1-423-475-7308
www.parsonsporch.com

Dedicated

to

Thomas J. Rainey, Sr.

Extraordinary Friend

and

Man of Prayer

Foreword

How does one say just the right thing at just the right moment? That, indeed, is the special gift of Dan Scott. Reverend Scott, Baylor School's Chaplain since 2003, has blessed our school family with special prayers in times of triumph and challenge, joy and sorrow. Somehow, through God's grace, Dan seems to find just the right words to comfort us and to lift us. Though he is a Baptist preacher, Dan's prayers reach across denominations and faiths to find their ways into the hearts of all. In God's name, he reaches out to all of us.

So we are proud to share some of Reverend Scott's prayers in this volume. We know that they will bless you just as they have blessed us. A grateful school says, "Thanks, Rev. Scott, for being who you are for us."

Scott Wilson '75
Headmaster

Prayer

Show us the way to fullness of life, O God:

- that our days at Baylor may be filled with joy, hope, and purpose;

- that we might respond to the opportunities before us;

- that we might be strengthened to face challenges;

- that we might learn to respect our brothers and sisters;

- that we might see the needs of others and give help;

- that we might become the persons we are called to be.

Hear our prayer today and every day.

Amen.

Celebration

Convocation and Installation of
Scott Wilson
August 26, 2009

Everlasting God,

You have been our guide for generations. By word and wisdom, reason and revelation, imagination and inspiration, You have led us to this very hour.

Now we ask for Your leadership for the challenges ahead.

Bring us to a new place. Help each one of us to set aside old failures, old grudges, old fears, and yes, even old successes, that we might plunge into the deep waters of new experience with faith and confidence.

We thank You for Scott and Susan Wilson. We are truly grateful for their willingness to lead.

- Walk with them as they walk
  with us.
- Encourage them as they
  encourage us.
- Inspire them as they inspire us.

May it one day be said of us that we did what was right and that our decisions were a reflection of Your guidance. Forgive us when we lower our standards to settle for less than our best. Open us as individuals and as a community to joy, service, and adventure.

Help us to make a positive difference here today even as we prepare to make a difference in the future.

We pray this prayer in the confidence of Your continued love and guidance.

Amen.

Opening Ceremony 2011

Eternal and Ever-Present God,

Thank You for the privilege of being in this place at this time.

Thank You for those who are here with us. Many of them will become our friends for a lifetime.

Thank You for your presence among us in all our conversations and interactions.

Now strengthen all of us for the journey ahead.

When we are down, lift us up.

When we are sad or upset, help us to be receptive to the encouragement of others.

When others around us are discouraged, may we become their encouragers.

Free us from our fears and anxieties about tomorrow. Let us be calm and confident and fully aware that You are always and forever with us and for us.

Hear our prayer.

Amen.

Awards Day 2006

God of our past, our present, and our future,

Today we stand on the shoulders of ordinary men and women who had an extraordinary vision.

We thank You for all those through the ages who have believed in the power of learning.

We thank You for our founders, who first gave life and spirit to this place.

We thank You for all those whose talents, gifts, and energies have kept their dream alive for generations.

We thank You for teachers who demanded from us our best and believed in us when we had little confidence in ourselves.

We thank You for parents and grandparents who have given and even sacrificed that we might pursue our dreams.

We thank You for our seniors, who have left their mark on our traditions and our hearts. Propel them now into tomorrow with confidence and exuberance. Keep their dreams alive even as they face their limitations.   Give them serendipitous experiences along the way. Show them how to be good and caring. Above all, help them to know Your great love for them.

And grant us all a sense of what it means to be community together, that we may truly be Your people.

Amen.

Recognition Day 2012

Eternal and Loving God,

We must begin with gratitude, for being truly thankful may be our greatest challenge when we have and expect so much. We are genuinely glad to be fully alive in this place and time.

... What a joy it is to be young <u>or</u> young at heart, to be eager and enthusiastic about life.

We are thankful for one another and for all that we have experienced together.

... What a privilege it is to be surrounded by friends, colleagues, and encouragers.

We are grateful for our differences.

... How exciting it is to celebrate the gifts and achievements of others.

We pray especially for our seniors as they continue their journeys beyond Baylor. Lead them to use both head and heart as they expand their world. Help them to get over high school, to move beyond the rewards and the failures, the successes and the slights, the pampering and the pain. Give us all the grace to forgive the people who were difficult or perhaps even damaging. May we hear and heed the advice of the Apostle Paul--"to forget what lies behind and strain forward to what lies ahead."

Remind us of what we already know: that there is a greater recognition to be achieved than anything we may applaud today. You have called us to a higher standard, the standard of active love. Our challenge is to see what others may miss--the hurting, the lonely, the abused, the forgotten--and to do what others may not do... to work to change this world... one person and one opportunity at a time.

Hear our prayer on this rewarding day!

Amen.

Awards Day 2012

God of every age and every stage of life, what we need to see is the big picture:

- bigger than the latest text or tweet,
- beyond simply who won and who lost,
- bolder than the newest style.

Open our eyes to see and know:

- that the universe is friendly,
- that we are deeply loved,
- that life is a remarkable gift,
- that our dreams can become reality.

Give our seniors faith and confidence as they face new challenges. May their achievements today be a prelude to an even greater tomorrow, and may our world be richer because of their accomplishments. Comfort them during the hard times. Help them to find the strength to battle their inner demons as well as life's great challenges. May they develop lasting relationships and a strong faith to guide their way. May they discover Your friendship through it all.

Today we are simply grateful. Where would we be without our encouragers--parents, grandparents, coaches, teachers, and friends who believed in us even when we had our doubts? We are especially grateful for the contributions of Schaack Van Deusen and David Harris. Oh how we will miss their laughter and their leadership. In retirement, grant them the satisfaction of a job well done plus new adventures and new delights.

Hear our prayer on this exciting day.

Amen.

Harrison Hall Dedication
May 8, 2009

God of the ages and of this good moment,
for generations people have heard Your voice and
your call:

- Your call to basic integrity,
- Your call to energetic service,
- Your call to exemplary leadership,
- Your call to joyful generosity.

Generations of Baylor families have taught us by
example that "to whom much is given, much is
required."

These strong men and women set the stage for this
moment. So today we stand on their shoulders,
grateful for their inspiration and awed by their
resourcefulness. They dreamed, planned, and labored
that Baylor might become a shining light and a place
of excellence.

We are grateful for all, who, by their giving, have
made Harrison Hall a reality.

We are grateful especially for the Harrison family,
who, by their faith and generosity, encourage
us all.

We are excited by the promise of this splendid gift.

May Harrison Hall become a special place:

- A place where faith is shared,
- A place where hope is restored,
- A place where strength is renewed,
- A place where community is formed.

Challenge and excite us with new dreams. Help our imaginations to soar. Save us from the human tendency to be timid and tepid as we attend to the future. Guide us to trust You, O God, so that our trust may lead us to obedience and our obedience to even greater generosity.

Now hear our prayer in the name of Jesus, who is God of our past, our present, and our future.

Amen.

Von D. Oehmig
Sports Performance Center
March 11, 2010

God of creativity and dreams,

We pause to give thanks... to express our gratitude to you.

- Gratitude for the generosity of all who made this facility possible;

- Gratitude for those whose imagination conceived it and whose ingenuity and energy brought it to completion;

- Gratitude for those whose dedication will make it useful and instructive;

- Gratitude especially for the Oehmig family, for their willingness to dream new dreams, for their faith in the future, and for their commitment to young people. They serve as an example to us all.

And now may the lessons learned here last a lifetime. May the young become strong in body and even stronger in character and spirit. And may we remember to be ever grateful to You, the source and resource of every good gift.

Amen.

Library Dedication 2011

Inspiring and Encouraging God,

We know You to be the God of words:

Spoken words, written words, words made flesh--the God of Torah and Testament and testimony.

Through words You inspire us, console us, and challenge us to high purpose.

May this be a place where words come alive in the minds and imaginations of our students.

We are thankful for those who teach and work in this space, for their helpfulness and their good humor. Encourage their work. May they find fulfillment in their endeavors, and may we be inspired by their dedication.

We are grateful for all those whose vision and generosity made this renewal a reality. Thank You for Bruce and his lasting legacy.

In the spirit of the Psalmist, "may the words of our mouth and the meditation of our heart be acceptable to You, O God, our rock and our redeemer."

Hear our prayer on this wonderful day.

Amen.

Zan Guerry Tennis Center 2012

God of every challenge and every opportunity,

We pause to give thanks for all that we see around us:

> --for the functional beauty of this facility...

> --and for those whose vision and generosity made it a reality.

But we also give thanks for all that we will see in the years ahead. With thought and imagination we can visualize lessons learned, friendships formed, talents developed, and victories won.

We are grateful for the stewardship of Zan Guerry and the tradition he has nurtured over time. We applaud his willingness to be a thoughtful, consistent, and cheerful giver. We are grateful for the Morgans and the Kadries, and we are inspired by their generosity.

As we enjoy this sport in this place, remind us that acts of love and service are not limited to any one opportunity. We are all called to make a difference in ways large and small, obvious and anonymous. Give us the insight and the desire to do what is good and truly helpful.

Now hear our prayer on this exciting day.

Amen.

Prayer for the Baylor Faculty 2011

Comforting and Challenging God,

As we prepare for the year ahead, we pause to ask for guidance and encouragement.

Surely we are in a holy place, not because we are assembled in this chapel, but because of the lives we influence. Remind us daily that labs and practice fields and classrooms are among the holiest places on earth. Let us remember that the word "teacher" is a holy word with holy responsibilities.

Help us to do what is best for our students, not just what is easy. Lead us to discover new ways to expand their horizons and their confidence. But as we work and teach, let us not neglect our relationships with one another.

Some among us are fighting difficult and lonely battles. We may be the adults in the room, but in so much of life, we are like children. We are learners and seekers. May we not take our opinions or ourselves too seriously. Give us moments of joy and help us to enjoy our moments. Show us the humor in things, and in ourselves.

Remind us that the rules of life apply to us. We too need rest and relaxation... fun and friendship... prayer and meditation. On some days, we just desperately need to laugh.

Bless and guide our leadership team this year. Give them wisdom and stamina. And give us all the willingness to work together.

Amen.

Prayer for the Baylor Faculty 2012

Creative and Instructive God,

Here we are once again preparing for a new year. Some of us are eager, others are anxious, but all of us desire to be effective at the tasks and challenges before us. So we ask that You do *to us* and *for us* and *with us* what we can never do alone.

Allow those who are new among us to relax and enjoy this year, but challenge those of us who are older not to relax too much. Keep our zest for life and learning fully alive. May we be just as curious at sixty as we were at twenty.

Help us all to grow throughout this year, to expand our emotional maturity as much as our intellect. At times we simply need to be quiet and to listen deeply to the viewpoints of others. At other times we should be more open, honest, and direct. Nudge us when we need to shut up and when we need to speak up.

Keep us safe from harm, even the harm that we may inflict upon ourselves. Remind us of our own humanity, our need for rest, relaxation, laughter, and a life beyond Baylor. Make us aware when negative thoughts and emotions are brooding in our minds and hearts. Save us from jealousy and envy and pettiness.

Remind us also of the humanity of our colleagues. Some among us even today have heavy hearts. Some of our students will begin this year deeply troubled.

Life isn't always easy or simple, so may we never ask more of others than is reasonable. Teach us how to season our expectations with a measure of grace and forgiveness.

Teach us the skills required for strong relationships. Even as we innovate and master our iPads, may we remember that mature and enduring relationships never go out of style.

Bless this year at Baylor. Encourage and strengthen our leadership team through every challenge. Extend our reach and our influence beyond anything we can imagine.

Amen!

Scholars Day 2009

Accept, O God, our thanks for all that you have done for us and among us.

We thank You for the splendor of the whole creation, for the wonder of life, and for the beauty of this place on this river.

We thank You for the blessing of family and friends, and for the loving care which surrounds us on every side.

We thank You for this day and all it represents. We thank You for tasks and challenges that demand our best efforts, and for leading us to accomplishments which bring satisfaction and delight.

Strengthen us now through the food we eat and the conversations we share.

Amen.

Comfort

Prayer for Tevin McKinney
(Death of his Father, Archie)

God of Comfort and Challenge,

We pray today for Tevin McKinney.

May our words and actions comfort him and encourage him, both now and during all his tomorrows.

We pray for others among us whose needs may not be so obvious but are just as real.

For the discouraged, the lonely, the angry... we pray.

Long ago You heard the prayers of people like us. Now let us relax in the confidence that You hear ours.

Amen.

Prayer for Janie and Eddie Davis

God of our hopes and our fears,

We come with our sadness and our concern to pray for Janie and Eddie, for their children, and for all who love them.

But we also come with our own frustrations, disappointments, and even anger to pray for ourselves.

Give to Janie what she will need for every hour.
Guide her medical team as they seek to diminish her pain.

Give to Eddie the inner strength to walk through this darkness. Give to us the continuing capacity to care for him.

If and when one kind of hope diminishes, sustain them with a higher and deeper hope.
If their faith falters, help us to be faith for them and with them.

But now we pray for ourselves.

We have seen enough cancer and pain and death... even here within our own community. We remember Joe and Ron, and we grieve.

We ask for answers. Teach us how to channel our frustrations into living hope.

Give our scientists and physicians greater insight and wisdom.

Give us as teachers the spark that might propel one of our own students to discover something so new and beneficial that it might be called a miracle.

Even this prayer reminds us that our human lives do not go on forever. Lead us to treasure life, to put aside the pettiness that so often consumes us, and to value every day and every relationship as an eternal gift.

Hear our prayer on this difficult but wonderful day.

Amen.

Tragedy at Virginia Tech 2007

God of Comfort and Challenge,

We pause this morning to pray for troubled people, both far and near.

We pray for the troubled community at Virginia Tech.

In the midst of their sorrow, sadness, confusion, and anger,
> --inject a measure of comfort.

For mothers, fathers, brothers, and sisters who have lost so much,
> --bring a moment of hope.

We also pray for troubled people much closer to home.

When those around us are troubled, give us the words, the wisdom, and the willingness to respond.

When we are troubled, save us from despair and silence and lonely self-destruction.

Remind us that we have someone to talk to and turn to. Remind us that we need not hurt alone.

We pray for our troubled world and even our own troubled society. Give us the insight to connect the dots between the seeds we sow and the society we reap.

Thank You for one another.

Thank You for our community.

Thank You for random acts of kindness experienced here every day.

Thank You for the privilege of prayer.

In the name of the one who calls us all to courage and kindness,

Amen.

Shipley Buckner

A year ago we lost a friend and fellow student, Shipley Buckner.

Today we pause to remember her.

It occurs to me that we must not remember simply to be sad, as if sadness alone could heal our sorrow. Many of you have lost people you love. You know that deep loss does not magically go away with a few tears. Our grief travels with us and becomes a part of who we are.

Today we remember Shipley as a unique person. We remember her personality, her style, her beauty, her humor. If you knew her well, you can probably close your eyes and see her and hear her. Maybe you can smile. Maybe you can even laugh.

We are all connected. We matter to each other. On some occasions, we know it. But most of the time we take each other for granted.

Today we also remember a tragedy. Life has enough tragedies... tornadoes, tsunamis, traffic accidents. How we respond to life's tragedies can make us or break us.

We must learn to go on... to live again after we are devastated by the tragedies we encounter. If she were here, I believe Shipley would tell you to go on into your exciting, challenging future with zest and determination.

One other thought... stay safe (as safe as possible). To know that you are vulnerable is to know a great truth. To consider the possible dangers ahead is neither weakness nor cowardice, but wisdom and maturity. I believe Shipley would tell you that as well.

Alumni Weekend

Walden Club 2011

Generous God,

We are surely thankful for the food we enjoy and the luxuries that are ours, but we are acutely aware that we do not live by bread alone.

We yearn for inspiration and imagination, hopes and dreams, challenges and accomplishments. Above all, we hunger for deep friendships along the way.

So give us tasks to do and people to love. Give us a vision for tomorrow. Give us the courage to start things that will bless the future far beyond us.

Thank You for Baylor and all that it has meant for generations.

Bless and encourage our leadership, our faculty, and most of all, our students. Thank you for our time together.

Hear our prayer.

Amen.

Challenge
(Football Game Prayers)

Saint Benedict School 2009

God of all our days,

At the end of this evening there will be winners and losers:

... some will be empowered and others will be disappointed.

We know that we need a larger perspective and a longer view.

Show us the way to a deeper joy than the temporary thrill of winning.

Take us beyond the thrill of victory *or* the agony of defeat.

Through all the ups and downs of life, in good times and bad, on sunny days and dark days, increase our contentment with the life we have.

At the end of this night and every night, may we echo the sentiments of the Apostle Paul...

"I have learned to be content whether winning or losing...I have found the recipe for happiness whatever I have or wherever I am"

On this night, we are thrilled to be here!

Amen!

Tyner High School 2010

God of us all,

We come to this moment with *gratitude*:

- for the beauty of this day and these incredible surroundings,

- for the excitement that is in the air and in us,

- for competition that makes us stronger and cooperation that makes us better,

- for teachers and coaches who challenge us, parents and grandparents who love us, friends who support us, and for faith that sustains us.

We are forever thankful.

Lead us now to do our best, to honor You, and to serve one another.

Amen.

Montgomery Bell Academy 2010

Good and gracious God,

In the beauty and excitement of this evening, we are reminded of Your constant creativity and generosity.

- You have lavished upon us both opportunities and resources.

- You have blessed us with a spirit of togetherness and friendship.

- You have given us the strength and ability to succeed.

Our lives are truly abundant, and we know that Your goodness and mercy have been our companions.

Because You are with us and within us, we are confident we can face any challenge before us.

We thank You for our schools, our traditions, and our students. Bless our coming and our going this evening, and hear our prayer.

Amen.

Brentwood Academy 2010

Eternal God,

We thank You for all that brings us to this place and time.

We thank You for families and friendships:

- for free assembly in a great nation,
- for the two institutions that claim our loyalties,
- for the gift of an inspiring education,
- for the thrill of competition and the joy of leisure.

But most of all, we thank You for our students who compete and cheer.

Teach them how to face all of life's challenges with optimism and determination.

Renew us now for life in this challenging world.

Help us to balance our lives, and free us, even for a few hours, from our fears and anxieties.

Teach us how to relax and enjoy the journey, even the detours, and fill us with the spirit and exuberance that comes from being fully alive.

Hear our prayer on this beautiful fall evening.

Amen.

The Ensworth School 2010

Encouraging God,

We admit that we often want more than we have: more success, more security, more achievement, and yes, even more victories.

So help us to channel our competitive instincts into those challenges that will make a positive impact on us and on our world.

Lead us toward those things that matter most.

Save us from small agendas and trivial pursuits.

Teach us how to be content... even as we strive for excellence.

May we truly give *our best* for *the best.*

Now bless us as we play and watch and cheer!

Hear our prayer on this beautiful and exciting evening.

Amen.

Battle Ground Academy 2010

God of every adventure and every experience,

Thank You for exciting moments that remind us that life is a grand privilege.

Thank You for moments of wonder and awe that reveal the grandeur of life.

Thank You for challenging moments that test our resolve and make us strong.

Thank You for moments of insight and inspiration that enable us to learn and to grow.

Thank You for defining moments that build our character.

Thank You for funny, even silly, moments that make us laugh and let us relax.

Thank You for quiet moments that allow us to reflect and breathe.

Thank You for emotional moments that remind us that we are human and needy.

Thank You for this moment... this time, this place, this challenge.

Let us rejoice and be glad in it!

Amen!

The McCallie School 2010

God of our hopes and dreams,

At the end of this evening, some of us will go home disappointed, and others will depart delighted, but whatever the outcome, we will move on to the challenges and opportunities before us. Thank You for always pushing us forward.

Help us to keep life in perspective:

- to know what is important and what is passing,

- to know what is permanent and what is temporary.

Lead us to tackle the difficult challenges and to run with confidence and joy the race that is before us. Make us stronger and better and bolder every day.

On this week when we honor our veterans, we pause to remember all those who sacrificed for our well-being. Some were our own parents and grandparents. Others were mentors and encouragers. Many are unknown and part of history.

Thank You for their character, their courage, and their endurance.

Now hear our prayer as we prepare for an exciting evening.

Amen.

Soddy Daisy High School 2011

God of every season,

We pause to be grateful for all the joys of life and especially the joys of summer.

Even in the scorching heat, we relished our time off. We enjoyed our time with family and old friends, our time to relax and reflect, our time to travel and explore.

But now we sense the excitement of a new season with new challenges, new opportunities, and new friends.

Open us to all that is ahead of us.

Free us from our fears and anxieties about the future.

In an age when we often describe the wonders around us as "smokin hot," we are thankful for our two "smokin hot schools" and our "smokin hot teams" tonight.

Bless us now as we play and cheer!

Amen.

The McCallie School 2011

God of every challenge,

As we assemble together again, we do so as thankful people...

- grateful for the deep loyalties this
    game represents;

- grateful for friends on both sides of
    this field;

- grateful for two traditions that
    strive to honor You through
    teaching and learning and serving.

Even though we are often fierce competitors, we are on the same team in our hopes and dreams for a stronger community and a better world. May we continue to bring out the best in each other.

So tonight, keep us safe, sane, and somewhat sensible. Forgive us when our exuberance becomes irrational or destructive.

Teach us how to play with head and heart.

And bless us all as we compete and cheer!

Amen.

Battle Ground Academy 2011

Ever-Challenging God,

When things go our way, we are up, but when things do not go our way, we are so often down. Even as spectators we sometimes lose sight of the bigger picture.

Help us to grow to be stronger people, with balance and perspective. Lead us to compete with grace and maturity. Teach us how to model both success and failure for all who look to us for guidance and direction, and always to turn our disappointments into determination.

On this night, we are grateful for our seniors. We are thankful for their dedication and the tradition of excellence they inspire. Encourage them as they continue their journeys. May they take the best lessons from this game into the larger challenges of life.

We pray for both teams that compete on this field. Keep them as safe as possible, and keep all of us secure in Your love.

Amen.

Christian Brothers High School 2011

Ever-Present God,

The nights are cool now. Fall is upon us. Winter is coming. Life is constantly moving and changing. And yet, in the midst of all that changes, you are our Rock, our Hope, and a stable Presence through all uncertainty. Help us to be fully alive and fully aware that You are always and forever with us. Teach us how to relax and enjoy life because of our confidence in You and Your confidence in us.

Thank You for our time together as we celebrate the successes of our students and friends. Keep them safe from all harm. Make this contest a teachable moment. May our students relish this moment that it might become one more building block toward a life of high purpose.

Make us fully grateful as we celebrate Thanksgiving with family and friends, aware of all we have and aware of what others need.

Amen.

Bradley Central High School 2012

God of the Young and the Young at Heart,

We have gathered for football, but in truth, we are here for so much more.

We are here because we love our children and because we know the power of support and encouragement.

We are here because we believe in young people, not only for their potential, but also for the zest they add to all our lives each and every day.

We are here because we know that the lessons learned in athletic competition will prepare our students for the ups and downs of life.

We are here because we believe in strong communities. We are better when we pull together as great teams always do.

So we ask that You bless our two teams and our two communities. Keep us safe and secure.

Hear our prayer on this beautiful and exciting evening.

Amen.

Father Ryan High School 2012

Eternal and Caring God,

So often on this campus we are awed by the beauty of
the earth. The mountains around us, the river below
us, and the trees above us make us want to shout for
joy.

But tonight we are aware that many of our fellow
citizens are finding that living on this earth can be
quite a challenge. We pray for those whose well-
being has been damaged by storms and circumstances
beyond their control. Strengthen their hope and their
resolve as they strive to rebuild their lives. And make
us all instruments of care and concern for a wider
community.

Teach us how to help those who struggle. May their
concerns become our concerns. Give us a willingness
to open our eyes and our pocketbooks, and challenge
us to give of our time so that no one will feel totally
alone.

We give thanks for the two institutions that are
represented on this field tonight and the faith
traditions that gave them birth and now offer them
guidance. May we be as good as our reputations!
Protect our players; guide our coaches, and remind us
that all of us have reasons to shout and cheer every
day.

Amen.

Montgomery Bell Academy 2012

In the beauty and excitement that surrounds us, O God, we turn to You as the source of all that we have and enjoy.

We are grateful for the many gifts on display this evening:

- for the strength and dedication of our players and coaches,

- for the enthusiasm of our cheerleaders,

- for the music from our band,

- for the loyalty of fans,

- for hands and voices behind the scenes that make tonight possible and enjoyable.

We are thankful for officials who attempt to keep our contests safe and fair.

We are even thankful for our opponents, without whom there would be no challenge or excitement.

So tonight, thank You for all these gifts and for each other.

Hear our prayer as we play and cheer!

Amen.

Brentwood Academy 2012

God of us all,

We like to believe that You are on our side.

But we also know that You are a big God--
so much larger than our preferences and prejudices.

Help us with our priorities. Give us the discernment
to separate the good from the best.

Thank You for the players, coaches, and fans here
tonight who know what is truly important. Thank
You for high standards. Thank You for inspiring
effort and dedication. Thank You for passion and
sportsmanship.

Remind us that You love us all, and for that reason
alone, we are all winners!

One final thought, O God--because You love us, we
wouldn't mind a few extra points!

Amen.

"Well God, we're here again--do something to us, for us, or with us."

www.ingramcontent.com/pod-product-compliance
Lightning Source LLC
Chambersburg PA
CBHW070206060426
42445CB00033B/1719